This is Your Life, Charlie Brown!

Selected Cartoons from IT'S A DOG'S LIFE,
CHARLIE BROWN, Vol. 1

Charles M. Schulz

CORONET BOOKS
Hodder Fawcett Ltd., London

Copyright © 1960, 1961, 1962, by United
Feature Syndicate Inc.
First published by Fawcett Publications
Inc., New York
Coronet edition 1968
Second Impression 1969
Third Impression 1969
Fourth Impression 1970
Fifth Impression 1972
Sixth Impression 1973
Seventh Impression 1974

Printed and bound in Great Britain for
Coronet Books,
Hodder Fawcett Ltd,
St. Paul's House, Warwick Lane,
London, EC4P 4AH
by Hazell Watson & Viney Ltd,
Aylesbury, Bucks

ISBN 0 340 04406 3

ARE YOU INTERESTED IN PEDIATRICS, CHARLIE BROWN?

LISTEN TO THIS..."SOME NEWBORN INFANTS ARE HIGHLY INFECTIOUS TO OTHERS, AND BECAUSE THEY ARE LITERALLY SURROUNDED BY CLOUDS OF BACTERIA, THEY ARE CALLED 'CLOUD BABIES.'"

WELL, WHAT ARE YOU LOOKING AT ME FOR?

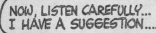

IS IT MORNING YET?

NO, IT'S ONLY TEN O'CLOCK.

TEN O'CLOCK?! GOOD GRIEF! THIS NIGHT IS GOING TO LAST FOREVER! I'LL NEVER MAKE IT! WHY DID LUCY HAVE TO BURY MY BLANKET? WHY?

ANYWAY, CHARLIE BROWN, IT'S NICE OF YOU TO SIT UP WITH ME THIS FIRST NIGHT.

THIS IS WHAT FRIENDS ARE FOR...

GOOD OL' CHARLIE BROWN!

HE'S FINALLY GONE TO SLEEP...

MAYBE IF HE CAN MAKE IT THROUGH THE NIGHT WITHOUT HIS BLANKET, HE'LL BE ALL RIGHT.

SLEEP IS WHAT HE NEEDS... IF HE CAN JUST SLEEP FOR...

WELL, HOW'S HE DOING?!

YOU THINK I'M BEING MEAN TO LINUS BECAUSE I BURIED HIS BLANKET, DON'T YOU?

WELL, I'M NOT! I'M REALLY DOING HIM A FAVOR! HE'S TOO WEAK EVER TO BREAK THE HABIT BY HIMSELF! HE'S AS WEAK AS... AS... WHY, HE'S AS WEAK AS YOU ARE, CHARLIE BROWN!

THAT'S A DISTURBING COMPARISON!

HERE'S A NICE PEBBLE, LINUS... TAKE IT HOME, AND OBSERVE IT.

THE FASCINATING THING ABOUT PEBBLES IS THEIR GROWTH, FOR SOME GROW UP TO BE STONES WHILE OTHERS GROW UP TO BE ROCKS...

YOU SHALL HOPE, OF COURSE, THAT IT GROWS UP TO BE A ROCK, FOR A PEBBLE THAT GROWS UP TO BE A STONE IS LIKE A YOUTH WHO HAS GONE ASTRAY!

✳SIGH✳ I HAVE SO MUCH TO LEARN!

"SOMETIMES HE WOULD STARTLE PEOPLE IN PUBLIC PLACES."

"HE FLEW OUT IN ANGER AGAINST ALL THAT WAS PETTY, DULL OR GREEDY IN MEN."

"...OFTEN, HOWEVER, HIS SCORN WOULD TURN TO HIGH HILARITY AND HUMOROUS JESTS."

ARE YOU READING ABOUT BEETHOVEN OR MORT SAHL?

DRAWING WITH CHALK ON THE SIDEWALK IS LOTS OF FUN!

IT'S REALLY A WONDERFUL MEDIUM...YOU CAN GET SOME VERY NICE EFFECTS...

I THINK IT RANKS RIGHT ALONGSIDE TEMPERA AND OIL AS AN ARTISTIC MEDIUM.

OF COURSE, IT HAS ITS DRAWBACKS, TOO

IT'S RATHER FRIGHTENING TO SEE THE DAYS GO BY SO FAST..

TO SAY THAT GRASS IS GREEN, YOU KNOW, IS NOT SAYING NEARLY ENOUGH...ACTUALLY, I'M VERY GRATEFUL FOR HAVING NATURALLY CURLY HAIR...I REALLY AM...

SOMETIMES MY DADDY CALLS ME "LADYBUG"....I USED TO READ A LOT, BUT LATELY I JUST DON'T SEEM TO HAVE TIME...

FRIEDA SITS BEHIND ME IN SCHOOL...I HAVEN'T HEARD A WORD OUR TEACHER HAS SAID THIS WHOLE SEMESTER!

FRIEDA, THIS IS MY SISTER, LUCY...

HOW DO YOU DO, LUCY? HAVE YOU EVER MET ANYONE BEFORE WHO HAS NATURALLY CURLY HAIR? ACTUALLY, I'M VERY GRATEFUL FOR IT!

SHE'S KIND OF A FRIEND OF MINE, LUCY, AND SHE SITS BEHIND ME AT SCHOOL....

PLEASE DON'T SLUG HER...

ONLY **78** MORE DAYS UNTIL BEETHOVEN'S BIRTHDAY!

THE OLDER YOU GET, THE FASTER TIME SEEMS TO GO BY!

THAT'S REALLY KIND OF DISILLUSIONING

WHAT'S THE MATTER?

SNOOPY ISN'T AS SMART AS I THOUGHT HE WAS...

HE MOVES HIS LIPS WHEN HE READS!

"DENTISTS MOSTLY AGREE THAT THUMBSUCKING **CAN** AFFECT THE SHAPE OF THE TEETH AND JAW...**HOWEVER**...

"..DENTISTS FURTHER AGREE THAT PSYCHOLOGICAL IMPLICATIONS INVOLVED IN PREVENTATIVE STEPS TO CORRECT THE HABIT OF THUMBSUCKING FAR OUTWEIGH THE ORAL PROBLEMS."

DENTISTS ARE A REMARKABLY UNDERSTANDING LOT!

THIS IS THE TIME OF YEAR WHEN I HAVE TO WORK THE HARDEST...

GETTING MY BASEBALL TEAM ORGANIZED IS A REAL JOB... THERE ARE A MILLION THINGS THAT HAVE TO BE DONE..

I HAVE TO NOTIFY ALL THE PLAYERS..I HAVE TO GATHER UP ALL THE EQUIPMENT..I EVEN HAVE TO SEE IF THE INFIELD NEEDS...

...MOWING!

I'M GLAD YOU'LL BE PLAYING SECOND BASE FOR US THIS YEAR, LINUS..

I'M ALSO GLAD TO SEE YOU HAVEN'T DRAGGED YOUR BLANKET OUT HERE WITH YOU...AFTER ALL, SECOND BASE IS NO PLACE FOR A BLANKET, IS IT?

MY BLANKET IS SECOND BASE!!

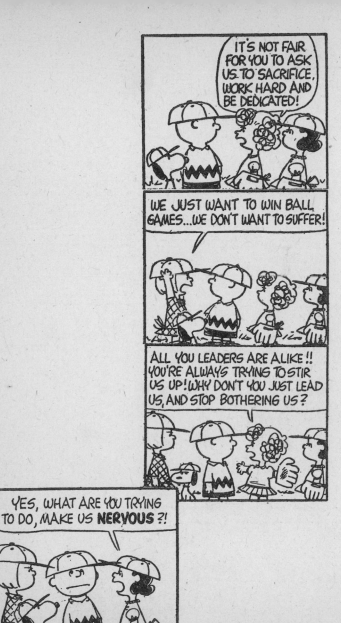

HEY, MANAGER, WE'RE AFRAID TO PUT OUR HANDS IN OUR GLOVES BECAUSE THERE MIGHT BE A SPIDER OR A BUG IN THERE!

OH, GOOD GRIEF! HOW DO THESE THINGS EVER GET STARTED?! HERE...LET ME PUT MY HAND IN FIRST JUST TO SHOW YOU THAT.

AAUGH!!

A BUG!

THANK YOU, MANAGER!

MONDAY IS OUR FIRST GAME, AND I FEEL LIKE LEAVING THE COUNTRY!

I'M JUST NOT CUT OUT TO BE A MANAGER, I GUESS...... MY SHOULDERS AREN'T BROAD ENOUGH.

YOU MEAN YOU'RE NOT READY TO ASSUME THE "MANTLE OF RESPONSIBILITY"?

BEFORE IT WILL FIT ME, THE "MANTLE OF RESPONSIBILITY" WILL NEED CONSIDERABLE ALTERATION!

WELL, LOOK HERE! A BIG YELLOW BUTTERFLY!

IT'S UNUSUAL TO SEE ONE THIS TIME OF YEAR UNLESS, OF COURSE, HE FLEW UP FROM BRAZIL... I'LL BET THAT'S IT!

THEY DO THAT SOMETIMES, YOU KNOW... THEY FLY UP FROM BRAZIL, AND THEY...

THIS IS NO BUTTERFLY... THIS IS A POTATO CHIP!

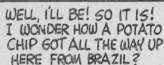

WELL, I'LL BE! SO IT IS! I WONDER HOW A POTATO CHIP GOT ALL THE WAY UP HERE FROM BRAZIL?

HOW CAN A PERSON JUST **DECIDE** WHAT HE'S GOING TO THINK?

DOESN'T HE HAVE TO THINK **FIRST**, AND THEN TRY TO DISCOVER WHAT IT IS THAT HE'S **THOUGHT**?

YOU'RE LOOKING AT ME WITH BLANK EYES!

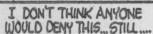

THEY'RE HAVING A GOOD TIME UP THERE ON THAT STAR TONIGHT.

IT LOOKS LIKE THEY'RE REALLY LIVING IT UP.

WHAT MAKES YOU THINK THAT?

THEY'VE GOT ALL THE LIGHTS ON!

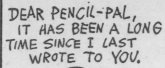

DEAR PENCIL-PAL, IT HAS BEEN A LONG TIME SINCE I LAST WROTE TO YOU.

I WOULD HAVE WRITTEN BEFORE, BUT I FORGOT ALL ABOUT YOU.

SOMEHOW THAT DOESN'T SOUND RIGHT...

LOOK, LUCY, WHY SHOULD ANYONE GIVE ANYONE ELSE A PRESENT ON BEETHOVEN'S BIRTHDAY?

WHY NOT KEEP IT SIMPLE? YOU HAVE A FEW FRIENDS OVER, HAVE A PIECE OF CAKE AND LISTEN TO THE NINTH SYMPHONY...

THAT'S A WONDERFUL WAY TO CELEBRATE BEETHOVEN'S BIRTHDAY!

ALL I WANTED WAS A PRESENT. WHAT DO I GET? A LECTURE ON HOW TO GIVE PARTIES!

And don't forget about all the other PEANUTS books in CORONET Book editions. Good Grief! More than THREE MILLION of them in paperback! See the check-list overleaf.

Wherever Paperbacks Are Sold

PEANUTS FOR EVERYBODY—FROM CORONET

CHARLES M. SCHULZ

All these books are available at your bookshop or newsagent, or can be ordered direct from the publisher. Just tick the titles you want and fill in the form below.

CORONET BOOKS, P.O. Box 11, Falmouth, Cornwall.

Please send cheque or postal order. No currency, and allow the following for postage and packing:
1 book – 10p, 2 books – 15p, 3 books – 20p, 4–5 books – 25p, 6–9 books – 4p per copy, 10–15 books – 2½p per copy, over 30 books free within the U.K.

Overseas – please allow 10p for the first book and 5p per copy for each additional book.

Name...

Address...

....